Dear Friends,

Our water supply is a precious one. As the uncertain future of our water develops, we must become more aware of our options to secure that future.

In Southern California 50% of our potable water is used for residential purposes. With a majority of our residential water being used for landscapes, alternatives need to be examined. In the entire state 77% of our freshwater is used for industrial agriculture. Growing food at home has been growing in popularity over the last few years.

Our Mediterranean climate like others in Australia, South America, Southern Africa, and around the Mediterranean Sea are biodiversity hotspots (Pimm and Jenkins, 2005) and habitat has been and is being destroyed at much greater rates than the tropical rainforests (Primack, 2010). Biologically diverse landscapes help reduce water needs of plants and increase biomass production (Tilman, 1999). Industrial agriculture in our area is partially responsible for desertification of our regions climate (Neff et al., 2005).

So, I encourage you to offset the food you buy by planting your own diverse food forest with Mediterranean Climate appropriate plants.

Whether your reason is to grow foods that are not available at the supermarket, whether it is to know where your food is coming from, or whether it is to offset desertification in our area, whatever it may be, I appreciate the awareness given to your landscape.

With this guide, you can not only grow your own food and help to improve water security and the environment, you'll also reduce your own water consumption with these plants.

Over the next few years I plan to continue searching for culinary plants and gathering as much information as possible, that is useful to you.

Stay tuned for a follow up edition that will have more plants such as the *Syzygium paniculatum*. We'll also have more cultivars for the species listed, with extended information on citrus, avocados, and grapes in particular. We'll also begin including more Southern California natives that have lost their uses over time.

I hope you find this guide useful and helpful. I myself am a local to the Southern California and my heart belongs to this climate. Like myself, all my research is born of this area, and I hope it provides for you what you are looking for.

Sincerely,

Andrew Kanzler

P.S.

It is important that you note that when these plants are described, they are indicated as being low, medium, or high "Dry Season Watering" plants. This means that once these plants are established (usually after their first year) they will only need additional water in summer months at low (once every few weeks to none at all) medium (once every other week) or high (once a week) amounts.

Trees

Acca sellowiana - **Pineapple Guava**

Parts used: Fruit, Flower Petals   Season: Autumn

The fruit, like the name suggests, is similar to a guava but tastes a bit like pineapple. It is a popular landscape plant in Southern California due to its low water usage. The flower petals taste like bubble gum and are extremely popular with children. The petals will do well in salads. Native to highlands of South America, this tree is sometimes grown as a large shrub.

Pineapple Guava

Size: 15-25 ft

Dry Season Watering: Low

Full Sun

Evergreen

Arbutus spp. - Strawberry Tree

Parts used: Fruit   Season: Summer

This slow growing tree is native to the Mediterranean region. The fruit only superficially resemble the strawberry. It is a popular landscaping tree and is beautiful when fully grown. The fruit themselves are not full of flavor, but they are edible. Occasionally you'll pick a fruit that is flavorful, but it is not a guarantee. The more common tree is the **Arbutus unedo**, the **Arbutus marina** is developing in popularity because of their more attractive blooms and better overall health.

Arbutus unedo

Size: 25 ft

Dry Season Watering: Low

Full Sun

Evergreen

Butia capita - Jelly Palm

Parts used: Fruit, Sap   Season: Spring

This is a feather palm native to South America. At one point it was a popular landscape plant in the U.S. The fruit is often eaten but some do not agree with its texture and strong flavor. The sap has been used to make wine, but it may be difficult to acquire. This palm may be more difficult to find in nurseries, but there are still growers out there that supply the palm. Can be seen at the Huntington Library in Pasadena

Butia capitata (Photo by: Megan E. Hansen)

Size: 20-25 ft

Dry Season Watering: Low

Full Sun

Evergreen

Citrus spp. - **Citrus**

Parts used: Fruit   Season: Winter/Spring

Citrus include Oranges, Lemons, Grapefruit, Kumquat, Lime and Tangerines (Mandarins). An extremely popular fruit and with a lot of history in Southern California. Many people are not aware, but these trees do not require a ton of water. Though they are native to the subtropics and tropics of Asia, they tend to do well here because of their long history of cultivation in the Mediterranean. In summer months they will require monthly deep watering. You'll know if your citrus are receiving too much water if their leaves begin to curl. There are a lot of varieties with new varieties being released every year.

Navel Orange tree wasting fruit

Size: 25 ft

Dry Season Watering: High

Full Sun

Evergreen

Diospyros kaki - **Persimmon**

Parts used: Fruit   Season: Autumn

Persimmons are native to North America and Asia. Many of the fruits are astringent until completely ripe, so you'll feel like you've taken a bite out of some cotton. The Fuyu Persimmon is a non-astringent variety and one of the most popular due to its smaller tree size and good fruit quality. Trees from the *Diospyros* genus have many uses and a variety of fruits, but the more common fruits are the Persimmons. Other species from *Diospyros* have delicious fruits and are also the main source of ebony wood.

Fuyu persimmons (Photo by: Koshy Koshy)

Size: 25 ft

Dry Season Watering: Low, Medium

Full Sun

Deciduous

Dovyalis caffra - **Kei Apple**

Parts used: Fruit   Season: Summer

This tree is native to southern Africa and its Mediterranean climate. The fruit is often a bright yellow or orange about one to two inches in size with several small seeds. Its flavor is similar to the apple and is juicy and often acidic. The trees themselves have long narrow thorns and require both female and male plants to produce fruit. They have recently been gaining some attention, but are still largely not available in many nurseries. Sometimes grown as a large shrub. Can be seen at the Wild Animal Park in San Diego.

Caffra fruit (Photo by: Tony Rolkins)

Size: 20 ft

Dry Season Watering: Low

Full Sun

Evergreen

Eriobotrya japonica - **Loquat**

Parts used: Fruit   Season: Spring

This is a common landscape tree in Southern California. Its yellow fruit are usually about one to two inches in size and are delicious. It has a small pit and is eaten like a cherry. It is often also called a Japanese Medlar or a Chinese Plum. It has become naturalized in the entire Mediterranean Basin and is a great tree for our area. It is a significantly important tree in Asia and is easy to locate in nurseries in California. Loquat trees will often grow slowly without additional fertilizer.

Young loquat with young fruit

Size: 15-35 ft

Dry Season Watering: Low

Full Sun

Evergreen

Ficus carica - **Common Fig**

Parts used: Fruit   Season: Summer/Autumn

The fig is a native to the Middle East. Its popular fruit
is used in cooking and is eaten fresh off the tree. It is a
common fruit tree and easy to find. The fruit does not
handle shipping well which make figs less common in
supermarkets. The sap gives off a white latex which has
industrial applications. Some people can have allergic
reactions to the latex. This tree seeds fairly easily and
volunteers will sometimes begin to grow. Most of the time
however, these volunteers are hybrids with fruit that is
nearly inedible.

Black Mission figs (Photo by: Monica Arellano-Ongpin)

Size: 9-35 ft

Dry Season Watering: Low

Full Sun

Deciduous

Macadamia spp. - **Macadamia**

Parts used: Nut   Season: Year round

Only two of the nine species in the genus contain edible nuts: the **Macadamia integrifolia** and the **Macadamia tetraphylla**. These trees can reach up to 50 ft. but usually do not spread. It can take 7-10 years before you will see many nuts in most varieties. The trees have spiny leaf margins and can be messy especially if the nuts aren't harvested often. One tree can provide a large harvest. The Macadamia nut shells are extremely hard and a hammer or a vise is often needed to de-shell the nuts. Can be seen at Cal Poly Pomona.

Macadamia in bloom

Size: Up to 50 ft high and only 20 ft wide

Dry Season Watering: Medium

Full Sun

Evergreen

Mespilus germanica - **Medlar**

Parts used: Fruit   Season: Spring

A native to the Middle East, this once common fruit in the U.S. is still eaten in Europe and the Middle East. Over the years the fruit began to lose its popularity and is largely unseen in American nurseries. The fruit is usually about one to two inches in size and the flesh is sucked out of its skin. It is often compared to apple sauce. In order for the fruit to ripen, the fruits will need to have adequate chill or be frozen before they start to soften up. Some suggest we may see a resurgence in the popularity of this fruit.

Medlar fruit (Photo by: Nick Saltmarsh)

Size: 10 ft

Dry Season Watering: Low, Medium

Full Sun

Deciduous

Morus spp. - Mulberry

Parts used: Fruit   Season: Summer

The silkworm from which we harvest all our silk from only eats leaves off of this fast growing tree. Many trees of this species become quite large and are often topped due to a homeowner not expecting such a massive tree in such a short time. There are different varieties however that stay small and can be used as alternatives. This tasty fruit is commonly eaten in Asia and the Middle East. The U.S. has its own native, but the fruit are still not common in markets. The large varieties of these trees are easy to find in nurseries. Ask around and you'll be able to find smaller species.

Pakistani Mulberry fruit (Photo by: Eric Schmuttenmaer)

Size: 15-65 ft

Dry Season Watering: Medium, High

Full Sun

Deciduous (Evergreen where Winters are warm enough)

Olea europea - Olive

Parts used: Fruit   Season: Summer/Autumn

The olive is native to the Mediterranean region. The fruit is generally not edible when fresh and must be pickled or prepared before eating. The oil from its seed is one of the most prized cooking oils but it is not something that can be easily extracted in the home. Most olive trees available at nurseries are not cultivated for their fruit. Some are also sprayed to prevent them from fruiting. They are a popular landscape plant for aesthetics, their fruit can be very messy and are often sprayed to prevent fruiting. Ask around and you'll be able to find some culinary types.

Olive tree

Size: 15-35 ft

Dry Season Watering: Low

Full Sun

Evergreen

Persea americana - **Avocado**

Parts used: Fruit   Season: Spring-Autumn

Not all Avocados are created equal. There are many avocado trees that will not do well in our area either due to cold weather or a lack of water. However, those cultivars are generally not available in nurseries in Southern California. These trees vary in size and in fruiting periods. They can be kept small, and it is suggested to have two types (A type and B type) to improve pollination. Leaf tips will often brown in our area because of salty soils During heavy rains, New leaves will not have brown tips.

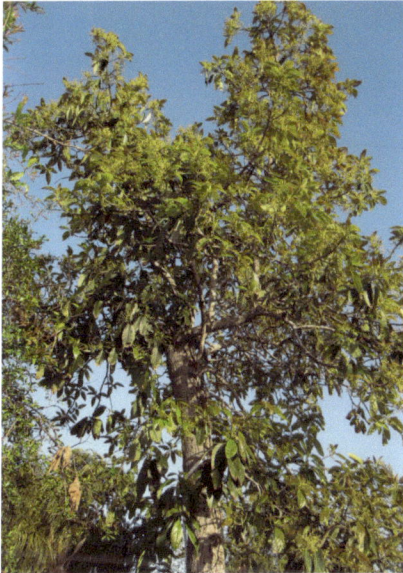

Bacon Avocado tree a narrow upright grower

Size: 9-35 ft

Dry Season Watering: Medium

Full Sun

Evergreen

Phoenix dactylifera - Date Palm

Parts used: Fruit   Season: Autumn

From the Middle East, this fruit is a staple of the Middle Eastern diet. Dates are an oblong fruit that contain a single large seed. This tree is a popular landscape palm, and in recent years has been seeing a lot of use. However, the type being used in landscapes is not a culinary type. Culinary types will need at least one male to pollinate the others for fruit. The fruit is delicious and often dried for storage. It is popular in salads, on its own and in cooking.

Dates in a Date Palm canopy (Photo by: Thierry Meurgues)

Size: 50-85 ft

Dry Season Watering: Low

Full Sun

Evergreen

Psidium spp. - Guava

Parts used: Fruit   Season: Summer/Autumn

Like the Avocado, not all guavas are appropriate for our climate and for the same reasons. Some may need more water and some may need protection from cold. The two most popular types are the **Strawberry Guava** and the **Lemon Guava** both of the *Psidium littorale* species. These two species generally stay below 15 ft and have one to two inch tasty fruits. They are delicious fresh or in smoothies.

Lemon Guava tree

Size: 10 ft

Dry Season Watering: Low

Full Sun

Deciduous

Punica granatum - **Pomegranate**

Parts used: Fruit   Season: Autumn

Another Middle Eastern native, the Pomegranate has seen a lot of use in juices in recent years as a superfruit. Pomegranates have been widely cultivated in the Mediterranean for many years. The fruit contains hundreds of small seeds with each seed surrounded by its own delicious pulp. The tree has long skinny thorns but it makes a beautiful landscape plant. Often grown as a large shrub, the flowers attract bees, birds and butterflies during the spring. The fruits vary from tart varieties to sweet varieties and clear pulp to dark red that can leave stains.

Wonderful Pomegranate trained as a single trunk tree

Size: 10 ft

Dry Season Watering: Low

Full Sun

Deciduous

Sambucus nigra - **Elderberry**

Parts used: Fruit   Season: Summer

The native elderberry is dark blue and covered in a white powder that make it appear to be a sky blue. Only when fruits have become blue are they safe to eat. A popular fruit for indigenous groups, it has not kept up with recent times. The berries are used to make pies and jam. The berries themselves are not very complex in flavor so lemon juice is often added to give it a little more to be craved. Out of hand they are sweet and delicious. European varieties are often used to make delicious wines. Elderberries have been proven to be effective in fighting flu symptoms.

The native Elderberry in bloom

Size: 10-15 ft

Dry Season Watering: Low

Full-Part Sun

Deciduous

Ziziphus jujuba - **Jujube (Asian Date)**

Parts used: Fruit   Season: Autumn

The Jujube is a delicious fruit similar to the Date Palm. This
fruit however, does not come from a palm tree, nor does
it have a large pit. The erect columnar trees leaves turn
a bright yellow when going deciduous and make a great
landscape tree for that reason. The fruit is ripe once it is half
brown, once dried it is very similar to the common date.

Jujubes (Photo by: Kristen Taylor)

Size: 15-20 ft, narrow upright

Dry Season Watering: Low

Full Sun

Deciduous

Shrubs and Groundcovers

Artemisia spp. - **Wormwood**

Parts used: Foliage   Season: Year round

There are many types of Artemisia and some are native, the extremely fragrant leaves are often used in cooking or as a garnish. The most common of this genus for cooking is the ***Artemisia dracunculus* - Tarragon**. Tarragon is used in Mediterranean cooking and there even exists a Tarragon soda. Use it as an herb to improve some dishes at home. We have a native, the ***Artemisia californica* - California Sagebrush** that is also very fragrant.

Tarragon

Size: 1 ft

Dry Season Watering: Low

Full Sun

Evergreen

Cynara cardunculus - **Artichoke**

Parts used: Bud   Season: Spring/Summer

The artichoke is another Mediterranean native. The large shrub is available as an annual or a perennial plant. The flower buds are cut off of their stem before they have flowered and are boiled or steamed. The base of the flower bud leaves are then eaten and the artichoke heart is the most prized part of this food. If left to flower the bright purple flowers make a great landscape addition. Cooked Artichoke hearts are often preserved in olive oil or put together with spinach and cream and cheese to make a delicious dip.

Artichoke

Size: 6 ft

Dry Season Watering: Low

Full Sun

Evergreen

Foeniculum vulgare - **Fennel**

Parts used: Fruit, Bulb   Season: Summer

The Fennel fruit is often mistakenly referred to as the seed. The fruit is used like an herb for cooking for a refreshing anise flavor. The bulb of the fennel is also used like anise, however the bulb is often sweeter and more aromatic.
In many Mediterranean climates this plant has become naturalized. In parts of California some may consider it invasive. Dry the fruit and save them for a later use. Fennel pollen is also an expensive and hard to find herb. If you have your own plants, you may be able to collect and use the pollen yourself!

Fennel fruit

Size: 6 ft, narrow upright

Dry Season Watering: Low

Full Sun

Evergreen

Fragaria califonica - **California Strawberry**

Parts used: Fruit   Season: Spring/Summer

The famous strawberry has a native cousin. These low growing and spreading plants make great landscape additions especially in shady areas. The fruits are very small but are often much sweeter than the strawberries found in heavy cultivation. If you've never had a native strawberry it's worth a shot to grow some of these in your home.

Young California Strawberry

Size: 1 ft spreads by stolons

Dry Season Watering: Medium, High

Full Sun - Shade

Evergreen

Laurus nobilis - **Bay**   Season: Year round

Parts used: Foliage

The Bay leaf is used in many different types of cooking. The large fragrant leaves are wonderful for food when dried. The whole leaves are usually removed before serving, but may also be crushed before cooking. Bay leaves have been used for cooking for as long as there has been a recorded history. Bay leaves are sometimes added to olive oils for some subtle addition in flavor. It is a common landscape plant and sometimes grown as a small tree.

Bay leaves and flowers (Photo by: Julio Gaspar Reis)

Size: 6-10 ft

Dry Season Watering: Low

Full Sun

Evergreen

Lavandula spp. - Lavender

Parts used: Flower, Bud   Season: Spring/Summer

Lavender is an extremely popular and fragrant shrub. It is beautiful with long lasting flowers and its fragrance is well known all over the world. It is native to the Mediterranean. It is not generally used in cooking, but the flowers are sometimes candied or dried and ground up to be mixed with tea. It is an extremely popular source for apiarists to have their honeybees develop honey from. In the U.S. it is popular to make scones with lavender buds. It is a great herb to experiment with and it has been said to be a great pair with chocolate and goat milk products.

Field of Lavender

Size: 1-3 ft

Dry Season Watering: Low

Full Sun

Evergreen

Origanum spp. - Oregano

Parts used: Foliage   Season: Year round

Oregano is an extremely popular herb particularly in Italian and other Mediterranean cooking. It is aromatic and warm. It can be a strong powerful herb and should be used lightly if your dried oregano ends up being strong. In colder climates, oregano is not as powerful. It makes a great landscape plant and the groundcover types can be a wonderful lawn alternative.

Kaliteri Oregano

Size: 1 ft

Dry Season Watering: Low

Full Sun

Evergreen

Rosmarinus officinalis - **Rosemary**

Parts used: Foliage   Season: Year round

Another Mediterranean herb, Rosemary can be used fresh or dried. Pick new growth where the stems have not become woody yet. There are many different cultivars of rosemary with blue, violet, pink, or white flowers. Many different forms of the shrub exist including hanging, groundcover, and medium sized shrubs. They are great as a hedge as well and are wonderful in walkways where one might brush up against the foliage to release some of its aroma.

'Collingwood Ingram' Rosemary in bloom

Size: 3-6 ft

Dry Season Watering: Low, Medium

Full Sun

Evergreen

Salvia spp. - Sage

Parts used: Foliage   Season: Year round

There are many different types of Salvia or Sage all of which can be used for cooking. ***Salvia officinalis* - Garden Sage** is the most popular and well understood type for cooking. Sage is used as an herb with fatty meats. It is popular in the Middle East and the Mediterranean for cooking. There are many native Sages that can be used as well and may call for some experimenting in dishes. Sage may also have some medicinal uses that are currently under examination by scientists. Sage flowers are also very attractive and are great in any garden.

'Amethyst Bluff' Sage

Size: 1-6 ft

Dry Season Watering: Low

Full Sun

Evergreen

Thymus spp. - Thyme

Parts used: Foliage   Season: Year round

Thyme is another great Italian herb that is used across the
Mediterranean. This small shrub generally has tiny leaves
that are picked and dried for a later use. Some varieties do
not hold on to their aroma when cooked so be careful when
buying if you plan to use it in food. Thyme can also make a
great lawn alternative with its small soft leaves and bright
beautiful flowers. If used as a lawn, mow it once a year after
the flowers have been spent to keep it clean.

Lemon Thyme

Size: 1 ft

Dry Season Watering: Low

Full Sun

Evergreen

Vines

Lycium barbarum - Goji Berry

Parts used: Fruit   Season: Summer

This deciduous vine is native to the Himalayas. It is a popular dried fruit which is then cooked in Asia. It is considered a superfruit and has recently become widely available in Southern California nurseries. The small red fruits are also commonly known as the Wolfberry. They can be eaten fresh or dried. Dried berries also make a delicious tea.

Goji Berry flower

Size: 10 ft vine

Dry Season Watering: Low

Full Sun

Deciduous

Vitis spp. - Grape

Parts used: Fruit   Season: Summer/Autumn

Grapes originated from the Mediterranean region. It was domesticated thousands of years ago and the U.S. even has its own culinary native that is disease resistant: the Muscadine Grape. There is a native California grape that gets massive, but the fruits are small seedy and sour. Grapes in Southern California often end up succumbing to Pierce's Disease which is why they are not more popular. However UC Davis has recently been able to hybridize disease resistant varieties. These have not yet been releasei to the public yet. Muscadines need some additional irrigation.

Young Cabernet Sauvignon Grapes growing up a Pomegranate

Size: Varies

Dry Season Watering: Low

Full Sun

Deciduous

Cacti

Cereus peruvianus - **Cactus Apple**

Parts used: Fruit   Season: Summer

This native of Peru has been used for many years. It is a common landscape plant in Southern California and many people do not realize that the fruit is edible. Although called Cactus Apple because of its appearance, it is not eaten in the same manner. The rind is usually removed and the inside is eaten fresh or chilled, often with a spoon.

Peruvian Apple Cactus in bloom (Photo by: Pizzo Disevo)

Size: 10 ft

Dry Season Watering: Low

Full Sun

Evergreen

Hylocereus spp. - Dragon Fruit

Parts used: Fruit   Season: Summer

A popular fruit in South America and Asia, this cactus is of tropical origins. Three common types are the ***Hylocereus costaricensis, Hylocereus megalanthus,*** and ***Hylocereus undatus*** with red skin and red flesh, yellow skin and white flesh, and red skin and white flesh respectively. This fruit is gaining some popularity in North America and is eaten just like the Cactus Apple. This cactus is a vining cactus and needs support for growth. In its native habitat they are epiphytic and will sometimes grow on the trunk of a tree without being attached to the ground. Fruit is also often called Pitaya, and needs to be pollinated to produce.

Hylocereus costaricensis fruit (Photo by: Boo Lee)

Size: Epiphytic

Dry Season Watering: Low

Full Sun - Part Shade

Evergreen

Opuntia spp. - Prickly Pear

Parts used: Fruit, Young Foliage   Season: Spring/Summer

This is a native cactus throughout most of the Americas. The fruit is also known as tuna and the young foliage before it has had a chance to develop spines is also known as nopal. Both the fruit and young foliage are eaten. The sweet fruit will usually have spines and should be eaten with care. Use thick gloves to pick the fruit or remove them with a fork or some other tool. When eating the fruit you can use a fork to break open the skin and then eat the pulp inside. The seeds are sometimes hard similar to guava, but the fruit is tasty.

Prickly Pear cactus with some fruit

Size: 10 ft

Dry Season Watering: Low

Full Sun

Evergreen

Stenocereus spp. - Pitaya Agria

Parts used: Fruit   Season: Summer

This spiny erect cactus has a fruit that some consider to be superior to some of the other cactus fruits. This is likely due to some acidity that is lacking from the others. While dragonfruit is also called pitaya, this fruit has the added agria to its name for the acidity. The fruit have thorns that are thick and long and thus difficult to eat. It is often grown as an ornamental in dry regions but difficult to locate in Southern California. It is a slow growing cactus and it may be some time before you see any fruit. These reasons may be why it is not as popular as the others despite its flavor.

Stenocereus griseus

Size: 15 ft

Dry Season Watering: Low

Full Sun

Evergreen

Where can I see these plants growing?

Some of the less common plants have listed locations within the descriptions. Many of the plants are very common and can be seen all over the Southern California Landscape.

To see many of them in one place visit:

The Chino Creek Wetlands & Educational Park located at:
Inland Empire Utilities Agency
6075 Kimball Ave. Chino, CA 91708

and

The Lyle Center for Regenerative Studies located at:
California State Polytechnic University, Pomona
4105 W. University Dr. Pomona, CA 91768

Bibliography

1 Pimm, S.L. and Jenkins, C. 2005 Sustaining the variety of life. *Scientific American* 293(33):66-73

2 Primack, R.B. 2010. *Essentials of conservation biology.* (5 ed., p 179). Sunderland, MA: Sinauer Associates Inc.

3 Tilman, D. 1999. The ecological consequences of change in biodiversity: a search for general principles. *Ecology* 80(5): 1455-1474

4 Neff, J.C., Reynolds, R.L., Belnap, J., Lamothe, P. 2005. Multidecadal impacts of grazing on soil physical and biogeochemical properties in southeast Utah. *Ecological Applications* 15(9): 87-95.

Photographic Credits:
Photographs with listed credits were licensed through the Creative Commons licensing agreements. These kind contributions and contributors do not sponsor the content or work created in this book in any way. All images were gathered on or before March 25th, 2012.